THE LAST CUPPA:
A One-Act Play

Ben Douglass

MERCURY FLATS PUBLISHING
Portland, Oregon. USA

FIRST EDITION

Copyright © 2026 by Ronald Dwayne Douglass

All rights reserved. No part of this book may be used or reproduced in any manner whatsoever, including professional or amateur stage productions, without written permission, except in the case of brief quotations embodied in critical articles and reviews. For information and royalty fees, email the publisher at:

mercuryflatsgazette@gmail.com

Library of Congress Control Number: 2026904561

ISBN: 979-8-234-00135-1 (Paperback Edition)

SAN: 992-3705

COVER: Generated by Microsoft 365 Copilot

Established 2014
Oregon Office of:

MERCURY FLATS PUBLISHING
(*An imprint of Atomic Mountain Press, LLC*)
5325 Northeast 37th Avenue
Portland, Oregon. 97211 USA

Printed in the United States of America

Synopsis of play

In a quiet tearoom somewhere in the Pacific Northwest, two old friends, Riley & Samuel, gather for what may be their final afternoon together. Riley and Samuel's friendship has survived the tests of time – decades of laughter, loss, and shared secrets. As they sip their tea, a dark cloud hovers over their heads: Riley has been diagnosed with stage 4 prostate cancer. Their conversation, gentle and unhurried, becomes a poignant exploration of memory, mortality, and the enduring ties that bind us together. This one-act play invites the audience to witness a moment of grace between two old men as they confront the inevitable, finding solace in companionship and the rituals of daily life.

Dramatist Personae

Riley – A once famous writer who was nominated for the Pulitzer Prize in literature, who is now long forgotten which nobody reads anymore. Now a frail, introspective old man, who is dying of prostate cancer, and seeks understanding and closure from an old friend.

Samuel – Riley's loyal friend, former publisher, and confident spanning decades, compassionate and curious, always willing to listen and challenge.

Ernest – Owner of the tearoom. Occasional presence, gentle and unobtrusive. Always smiling.

Story Notes

Setting – The Fern & Fable, a queer-owned tearoom somewhere in the Pacific Northwest. A cozy, botanical-themed spot where neighbors, friends and family gather. A place where one can get a simple breakfast, beverages, and enjoy the many plants for sale, as well as other New Age paraphernalia.

Time – The present.

Theme – Existential reflection, friendship and acceptance.

Production Notes

Props – A small table, two chairs, a half counter with tea pot, cups & saucers, bagels, napkins, etc. A colorful background showing a window with raindrops. Add green and colorful plants around the stage. An umbrella rack with several umbrellas in it. But keep the stage as minimalist as possible so as not to distract the audience attention away from the characters.

Lighting – The play takes place in the late afternoon so the lights should be subdued since its cloudy and raining outside. The lighting should reflect a somber mood.

Clothing – The two main characters should be dressed in the style of the Pacific Northwest, especially for the rain.

Dedication

Arthur "Tony" Joseph Marshall

1929 -2025

Who taught me the basics of dramatic writing and how not to give up until the project was done. A retired aerospace engineer who was a substitute math teacher during his retirement. He also wrote essays, newspaper articles and a novel called, *Bridge To Eternity*.

Acknowledgments

Thank you Rene Walsh of Walnut Creek, California for your expert final editing of this play. Also for the last minute suggestions on formatting. I could never have done it without you.

The following deeply inspired me to write this play and I acknowledge them here:

The movie, "My Dinner with Andre."

And the following dramatic plays:

"Waiting for Godot" by Beckett
"No Exit" by Sartre
"Ballyturk" by Walsh

Scene opens with Riley and Samuel sitting at a table next to a window, sharing a large pot of tea with bagels and cream cheese. Both are distracted by ice pellets hitting the window like gravel.

RILEY: [*Gazing out the window*] You know, Sam, there's comfort in places [*as he expands his arms*] like this tearoom. It's like visiting an old friend that will always be there when you need it. The world out there [*as he taps the window with his finger*] changes too much, but here, here it's as if time stops for a little while so you can catch up.

SAMUEL: [*Smiling softly*] Maybe that's why we keep coming back every week. Or maybe it's the awesome Russian Caravan tea we both like. Or the ambiance inside here. [*As he looks around the tearoom*].

RILEY: Or perhaps [*Letting loose with a big smile*]…it's the company.

SAMUEL: [*Looking serious*] How are you doing today?

RILEY: [*Looking out the window again*] You know, Sam, the doctor says my PSA levels and scans are way up beyond anything normal. A needle biopsy three days ago revealed 4th stage prostate cancer. At my age, I suppose it's almost expected.

SAMUEL: I hear you, Riley. Seems like the older we get, the more we collect doctors like baseball cards. I had my own scare last year – lucky it was just an enlarged prostate, not the big C. Still, it made me think long and hard.

RILEY: It sure does, my friend. I keep wondering: Why is it always something? We spend our youth worrying about the most trivial things, and later on it's our own bodies turning against us. I'm not afraid of dying, Sam, but I'd rather it wasn't drawn out and painful, like the stories I hear. I don't look forward laying in bed in hospice care all drugged up on morphine. Sometimes I think about using the Death With Dignity Act as my final exit strategy.

SAMUEL: Have you really given that some serious thought?

RILEY: Not really…

SAMUEL: None of us gets out of here alive, Riley, you know that. My father used to say, "Death and taxes are the only things we can really count on in life. Everything else is a damn turkey shoot." I've made my peace with it [*Long pause*] mostly. Cancer, heart disease, asthma, whatever – it's all just a matter of time when the grim reaper knocks on your door unexpectedly. But I'd like to stick around long enough to see my grandson graduate from university.

RILEY: Funny you mentioned peace. I sometimes think the fear is not death itself, but all the shit that comes before – the uncertainty, the loss of dignity, people avoiding you because they don't know what to do or say. They have no desire to feel your pain. I see guys in the waiting room, silent, staring out the window like they're searching for answers that never come, or planning an imaginary escape.

SAMUEL: It's true. You get to this stage and realize how much time you spent running from the idea of death. Your life becomes one distraction after another. Now, it sits with you like an old friend. [*Big sigh*] You know, Riley, I try to be grateful for every day, even the bad ones. What else can I do?

RILEY: Maybe that's the secret we all tend to overlook – gratitude. The chance to talk, to laugh, to remember, to hear the birds sing their songs, to plant a nice garden, to watch a kitten play with its tail. Even with prostate cancer staring me down, I find myself cherishing the small things now: the morning paper, petting my cat, a decent cup of tea, your company.

SAMUEL: It seems that's all we have, Riley. And when the time comes, I hope we can go as we lived -

- honestly, and with a bit of mirth. Let's just keep talking, and maybe the inevitable won't seem so grim.

RILEY: Agreed, my friend. Agreed.

SAMUEL: So what else is bothering you today? You seem especially lost!

RILEY: Exhaustion…mostly. But not just my body. There's an exhaustion deep in my soul, too. I suppose that's what old age offers us in abundance.

SAMUEL: Tell me about it. All these years, Riley, you've gathered so many experiences, stared life in the face without flinching. Maybe it's time to share some with me you've hidden away.

RILEY: [*Nods slowly*] Yes, I think I'd like that. [*Long pause*] It's funny how one begins to ponder one's life journey, as the end seems nearer than the beginning.

SAMUEL: I'm here. I'll listen. [*Puts hand across his heart*] Begin wherever you wish.

Ernest brings the two friends a fresh pot of Russian Caravan tea and two more bagels with cream cheese. He nods and smiles. Samuel pours Riley a fresh cup of tea and passes the small bottle of honey.

RILEY: [*Staring into his cup of tea*] You ever think, Sam, how quickly it was all over? One moment, we're chasing after dreams, the next – they're chasing us.

SAMUEL: [*Chuckles wryly*] I suppose time is the only real thing faster than the stories we used to tell ourselves and others.
But I don't dwell on it. Life happened. We lived it. Whether we had choices in the matter or not. No use in looking back with regret. Life still happens. We should be aware every moment.

RILEY: Not regret. More...wonder.

Wonder at what comes next. Do you ever find yourself lying awake in the dark, asking yourself if there's something beyond all this? [*He raises both palms upward in dramatic fashion*] A god? An afterlife? Reincarnation? Or whatever?

SAMUEL: [*Shrugs*] I used to, when I was younger and thought I could bargain with the universe somehow. Now? I suspect the end is just that – the end. Like the final page of a great novel you wish that would go on forever. [*He picks up his bagel, smears it with cream cheese, takes a big bite and chews with a thoughtful look on his face*]

RILEY: But great novels linger on, don't they? Their stories echo in memory. Maybe our lives do, too.
Perhaps there's something – somewhere – where our stories continue and thus we become immortal.

SAMUEL: [*After he puts three sugars in his tea cup, stirs, take a sip, he softens his tone*]

Maybe. Or maybe we become the stories others tell and pass on down generations. A laugh, a lesson learned, a warning. But as for the pearly gates, angels playing harps, streets paved with gold...I'm not convinced. Probably stories told to children to keep them distracted from the horrors of life.

RILEY: [*After long pause while sipping his tea*] Please. Continue. I'm quite interested.

SAMUEL: What happens after we die? It's the main question that has haunted us all ever since Gog and his mate sat around a fire inside a cave on a cold winters night. As a soft atheist, I don't believe in an afterlife, in beautiful realms beyond, or in souls ascending to a better place. To me, death is simply the end – an unceremonious conclusion to the story each of us writes with every thought, word and action we take. It's not a lake of hell fire, nor is it a grand adventure with angels blowing trumpets in the background on the other side. Like I said before, It's the end of a great novel, the last flicker of consciousness, and the return of our atoms to the universe. Folks often ask me if this belief – and it is certainly a belief – makes life meaningless. But for me, it is quite the opposite. If there's nothing waiting for us beyond this world, then every moment matters more. Every moment is precious. The love I share, the laughter I enjoy, the kindness I show, and the curiosity that drives me – they're all finite. There's no cosmic scoreboard, nor scorekeeper, tallying my deeds, no reward or punishment awaiting my words or actions. I am solely responsible for my choices, and the meaning I find is constructed in the here and now. I've heard the arguments over and over again: Heaven, Valhalla, or whatever provides one comfort, hope, and a sense of justice. But I find comfort in the natural order of things, in the cycles of birth, taxes and death, and in the idea that I am a tiny part of something vast and wonderful.

The universe doesn't owe me immortality, nor does it guarantee justice. Instead, it offers an opportunity – a very brief chance to exist, to learn, to connect, and to leave my mark in life, however small. When I contemplate what comes next, I feel a sense of peace and well-being. Not because I expect Heaven or Hell, but because I accept that my life is precious precisely because it is temporary. What comes next, for me, is not a place but a legacy: the memories I leave, the ideas I share, and the ripple effects of my actions. If my consciousness fades at death, then my impact lives on in the lives I've touched, the stories I've told, and the world I helped create. That's enough for me. So, when my time comes, I hope to have lived fully, loved deeply, and thought honestly. And if there is something after all, then let it surprise me. Until then, I will cherish the here and now, and let tomorrow remain a mystery.

RILEY: Wow. Just wow. [*He stares out the window for a few seconds*] I hope there's something, Sam, a reunion, a place where sickness and pain fade away forever, and we find those we've lost. Be it family, friends and even those pets we came to cherish and love. It comforts me, Sam, thinking that in the end we're much more than five pounds of minerals, fats, proteins and bone.

SAMUEL: [*Reaches across table and places a hand on Riley's shoulder*] You always did find hope in the smallest things, my friend. Maybe that's what makes this life of ours bearable – the hope, not scientific certainty. I'll settle for that. And I'll give you that. But please go on. Tell me more. Seems we got sidetracked about the great hereafter and all the stuff that implies.

RILEY: [*Takes a bite from his bagel, chews it slowly while looking at the ceiling, then a sip of tea and looks Samuel straight in the eye*]

I was a curious child. Always asking questions, getting into trouble with adults who didn't want to answer my questions or didn't know the answer, or how to react. My father said I had a restless mind, that dreamed beyond our small town, and needed to be tamed. My mother, however, told me many times I had the heart of a poet.

SAMUEL: And what did you dream about?

RILEY: Becoming a world famous journalist, mostly. I wanted to report from far off places like Tehran, Peking, French Congo, and tell the stories of the locals and their everyday troubles. I wanted to capture the world in words and make people feel the same emotions I did. But life had other plans for me. [*Smiles wistfully*] I also remember the huge apple orchard behind our house when I was three years old, endless in my mind. I thought I'd run forever through the rows of trees, unbound by fences, unafraid.

SAMUEL: Did you ever feel you could?

RILEY: For that moment, yes. Childhood lets you believe in endlessness. Then real life, like dusk, slowly settles upon you. Dreams change. Some fade away forever.

SAMUEL: But those dreams shape us, don't they? Even the ones that have faded away?

RILEY: Especially those. They teach us longing, and sometimes acceptance. [*The aromatic tea cools. Riley's hands tremble slightly and lets out with a big sigh as he recalls those difficult years.*]

ERNEST: [*From over at the counter he waves*] Hey you two. Is there anything else I can get you. A warm-up on tea?

Both Samuel and Riley wave Ernest off with smiles.

RILEY: [*Looking directly at Samuel once again*] There have been times when I lost my way. I tried and failed — more than once. My first book of poetry was rejected by every publisher from here to Timbuktu. Even the small presses didn't want it. That was a huge blow to my ego.

SAMUEL: Failure hurts. But you kept on going and managed some pretty big literary successes. Even getting nominated for a Pulitzer prize at the tender age of twenty-seven. You were a stubborn one back then. Each setback taught you humility and patience. That's when you concluded that the world didn't owe you dreams fulfilled.

RILEY: And then there was my marriage to Sofia…well, it didn't survive the storms I brought home. It's strange how a single event can unravel years of being together. When I hear people talking about divorce, they use words like "breakup", "separation", or "moving on" – but none of those seem big enough to describe what it feels like to lose your one true love. They make it sound so casual, like a change of address or a new job. But in reality, it feels as if your heart has exploded.

I remember the first time I saw Sofia. The way she smiled, the way the world seemed to tilt just a little, as if it was aligning itself just for us. That feeling, the certainty of true love, is rare. It's precious. We built a life together – side by side, dreaming and fighting and hoping. We believed that love would be enough. It wasn't. Having our daughter cemented our marriage for awhile. But after Petra left the nest, it just wasn't sustainable anymore. But we both learned that even love couldn't stand the storms that life tossed our way. The cracks came quietly at first: tired conversations, the silence after arguments, the feeling that we were drifting further apart, even while sitting together. The divorce papers were the final punch in the gut. Those papers being delivered felt unreal – the end of "us" and the beginning of "me." Now I'm haunted by memories. The way her singing filled the house, the warmth of her hand in mine, the simple joy of sharing a meal, even the silly fights about nothing. All gone. I don't just mourn the relationship, but the person who was my north star, the person who knew my soul backwards and forwards. Sometimes I think losing Sofia was the price I had to pay for having experienced it at all. Maybe some loves are meant to burn incredibly bright and then slowly fade away, leaving a scar that can never be forgotten. Divorce isn't just the end of a marriage. It's much more. It's a loss of shared dreams, of a shared future, and, for some of us, the loss of our one true love that can never be replaced.

SAMUEL: And now?
RILEY: [*Taking both palms and rubbing his eyes*] Now, I try to see the lessons learned, not just the regret.

Both friends pause and look out the window, listening to the ice pellets hitting the glass like gravel. In the background of the now empty tearoom, Ernest bustles about behind the counter. This goes on for over a minute.

ERNEST: [*He walks over to the table wiping his hands with a towel*] Hey guys. Nobody is showing up because of the crappy weather. I've decided to close early, but you still have forty-five minutes to sit and enjoy. [*He then smiles and walks back behind the counter*]

RILEY: [*Turns away from window, brightens up and looks directly at Samuel*] But there was joy, too. My daughter Petra's laughter echoing throughout the house, as she playfully chased our cat from room to room. The day my collected poems were published – one copy on a dusty shelf, but it was mine. All mine. Quiet afternoons with friends, like this, sharing stories and tea.

SAMUEL: You've touched lives with your poems, stories and plays, Riley. And just think, your one three act play – "Endurance," the one nominated for the Pulitzer, is still performed in high schools across the country to this day. You've touched more than you will ever know.

RILEY: [*Warmly*] And I've been touched in return. Love, friendship, small kindnesses – they matter far more than any literary achievements. Sometimes happiness hides in the ordinary, sometimes in front of your face. You just have to see it and then appreciate it.

SAMUEL: Maybe that's what we should chase – moments, not milestones.

RILEY: Wise words, Sam.

As the rain and sleet subside outside, both men take a break from talking and finish their bagels and tea. Then the conversation takes a brief philosophical turn.

RILEY: [*Checks his cell phone*] I spent years searching for life's meaning, reading, writing, learning, traveling. I wanted to know why we're here, what it all amounts to. I've sat in Zen temples across North America staring at blank walls; I've spent hours in prayer in Mosques throughout Asia;

I spent six months tending a vegetable garden at the Findhorn community in Scotland; I spent a year living among the Amish in Pennsylvania.

SAMUEL: Did you find any answers?

RILEY: [*Shakes head side to side*] Only more questions, Sam. [*Long pause as he drums fingers on the table*] I think self-realization isn't all it's cracked up to be. I found human frailty at every turn. It's the slow acceptance of what we are, and what we are not.

SAMUEL: Do you have regrets?

RILEY: Of course. But regrets are shadows – always behind us. We choose whether to face the sun or the darkness.

SAMUEL: You chose both, I think. That's what makes you real. That's what makes you human.

RILEY: Perhaps you're right, Sam. I'm still learning, even now.

Both men sit in silence for a few minutes. Riley's expression is pensive.

ERNEST: Ten more minutes, gents! [*As he smiles and waves behind the counter*]

RILEY: Sam, thank you for listening – for sharing these cups of tea and bagels, these pieces of life.

SAMUEL: You gave me more than stories, Riley. You gave me friendship, wisdom.

RILEY: And you reminded me that the journey matters more than the destination. I'm not afraid anymore. I can accept what's come and gone, and cherish what remains.

SAMUEL: Well, my friend, it seems the time has come to part ways once more. Hard to believe we've shared so many cups of tea together.

RILEY: Too many to count, Sam. But each one was worth it. I'll miss these afternoons – your stories and your questions and challenges.

SAMUEL: You know, the world has always felt a little less daunting with you as my friend.

RILEY: Even as we go our separate ways, those memories will stay with me somehow, someway, in another place, another time...I hope.

SAMUEL: Yes, to whatever may come...May it surprise us…

RILEY: Then let's raise a cuppa! To journey's, to acceptance, and especially to hope. [*He gives Samuel a big wink*]

SAMUEL: To hope!

The two men lift their cups and toast. Stage lights dim sharply. Curtain.

Finis

Two Old Friends, Memories, and Existential Angst – A Review of The Last Cuppa, A Play by Ben Douglass

By Rene Walsh

This one-act play by Mr. Ben Douglass centers on two elderly friends who share the past and confront personal existential angst. The dramatic tension is high because of the revelation that one of them is dying of prostate cancer, while the other attempts to comfort him. The plays brevity and intimacy allow for an intense exploration of mortality, regret, and the complexities of human connection.

The play unfolds in a cozy tearoom somewhere in the Pacific Northwest, probably Portland if my guess is right. The one-act structure with only one continuous scene compresses time, forcing the characters to confront their emotions without distraction or escape. Since there is only one other minor character in the background, the dialogue on the interplay between memory and impending loss is front and center.

The dying man – Riley – faces stage four prostate cancer and is confronted with his own mortality. His memories are tinged with regret, nostalgia, and the urgency of his impending death. His angst may stem from an unresolved relationship, unfulfilled ambition, or fear of oblivion and being forgotten. His vulnerability is exposed, making his memories both a comfort and a source of spiritual pain.

The comforter – Samuel – though not facing imminent death, is still grappling with his own aging and mortality. His attempts to soothe his friend might appear awkward, tender, or even desperate. He might share memories or distract his friend from pain, but he is also forced to confront his own fears and inadequacies.

The themes are many in this short play but powerful in themselves.

The play confronts death directly. Riley's fatal diagnosis is not just a plot device but a catalyst for reflection and honesty. The memories shared serve as both solace and torment. The men recall moments of joy, regret, and loss, illustrating how the past shapes their present. Riley's personal angst may revolve around things left unsaid or undone. Samuel's own angst surfaces as he realizes he cannot fully ease his friends suffering. The play also explores the limits and power of friendship. Consolation is imperfect, but the act of sharing memories and presence is meaningful.

The language of the play is understated, with moments of tenderness and raw honesty. Silence may play a significant role, as the men struggle to articulate feelings that words cannot capture. Riley may express frustration, fear, or simple resignation, while Samuel tries to offer hope, distraction, or companionship.

Even the mundane serves as symbols of memory and loss in this play. The ever happy and smiling Ernest is a symbol of youth and hope. The diagnosis itself could symbolize not only physical decline but also the inevitable passage of time, affecting both men.

This play provides a very poignant exploration of aging, mortality, and the bonds that sustain us. By focusing on two old friends sharing memories and confronting personal angst, Mr. Douglass invites the audience to witness the fragility and resilience of human connection. Samuel's attempts to soothe, though imperfect, underscore the importance of presence and empathy in the face of suffering. Ultimately, the play reminds us that consolation is found not in answers, but in shared experience and honest companionship.

Acting Rights/Permissions

CAUTION: Professionals are hereby warned that THE LAST CUPPA is subject to a royalty of $2,500.00. It is fully protected under the copyright laws of the United States of America, and of all countries covered by the International Copyright Union (including the Dominion of Canada and the rest of the British Commonwealth), and of all countries covered by the Pan-American Copyright Convention and the Universal Copyright Convention, and of all countries with which the United States has reciprocal copyright relations. All rights, including professional, amateur, motion picture, recitation, lecturing, public reading, radio broadcasting, television, Internet, social medias, and the rights of translation into foreign languages, are strictly reserved. Particular emphasis is laid upon the question of readings, permission for which must be secured directly from the author or MERCURY FLATS PUBLISHING in writing or email.

The royalty fee for amateur community theater, high schools, community colleges, religious organizations, and churches are set at $100.00.

All inquires should be sent to the publisher at:

mercuryflatsgazette@gmail.com

OR the author at:

mercuryflatsgazette@gmail.com

About the Author

For the past 44 years, the author has lived in Portland, Oregon. The last 38 of those years, he has resided in the Concordia neighborhood of Northeast Portland, with his partner, Ave Marie, and currently one dog and four cats.

Ben Douglass was born and raised in Napa, California until age 6, when his family moved to Hayward, California, where he graduated from Hayward High School in 1974.

He has held the following jobs in his long and varied working life: church janitor, burger flipper, tannery worker, leather coat factory cutter, mechanics helper at a garment factory, high-rise armed security officer, suicide hot line worker, street youth outreach worker, transitional housing coordinator, assessment/intake counselor at a methadone maintenance clinic, and finally, a 20-plus year run as a grocery worker and manager. The author is now retired.

The author has never stopped his continuing academic education, for he believes a culturally made person must keep learning until the day we die. He holds certificates in technical writing, creative writing, poetry, and an undergraduate certificate in systemic family therapy.

Publications By Author

The author has numerous "self-published" works under the Mercury Flats Publishing moniker. These are:

Confession of a Former Zombie: A Memoir (Paperback) Copyright 2014
ISBN: 13: 978-1500586515
ISBN: 10: 150058651X
Genre: Memoir

This Ain't the Waldorf Astoria, Honey! (Paperback) Copyright 2017
ISBN – 13: 978-1537082707
ISBN – 10: 1537082701
Genre: Novella

Beneath The Surface (Paperback) Copyright 2020
ISBN: 978-0-578-79355-9
Genre: Poetry Collection

The author has many kindle short stories that are too many to list here. Also self-published.

The author also has had numerous works published by the small press, Atomic Mountain Press based in Kashi Hara, Nara Ken, Japan. The most notable of these is:

Milking The Beast Within (Paperback)
Copyright 2021
ISBN: 978-0-578-97972-4
Genre: Poetry Collection

ABOUT **MERCURY FLATS PUBLISHING, ABN**

Dedicated to reprinting forgotten works by various misfits, outsiders, and rebels. Also, to highlight the works of new independent authors who want nothing to do with the big corporate publishers. The underlying concept here is based on a few simple propositions:

A) That to be a success under the current definition is highly toxic – wealth, fame and power are a poison cocktail;
B) That this era of triumphal capitalism glorifies the dreariest human traits like greed and self-interest as good and natural;
C) That the "winners" version of reality and history is deeply lame and soul-rotting stuff.

Given this, it follows that the truly interesting and meaningful lives and real adventures are only to be had on the margins of what Kenneth Rexroth called "the social lie."

It's with the dropouts, misfits, dissidents, renegades and revolutionaries, against the grain, between the cracks and among the enemies of the state that the good stuff can be found.

Fortunately, there is a mighty subterranean river of testimony from the disaffected, a large cache of hidden history, of public secrets overlooked by the drab conventional wisdom the **MERCURY FLATS PUBLISHING** aims to tap into. A little something to set against the crushed hopes, mountains of corpses, and commodification of everything. We think, it's the best thing Western Civilization has going for itself.

Tahoma Font - Usage/Design/History/

This font and the 14-point size was deliberately used in this publication for "easy reading" and to help those disadvantaged folks with sight problems.

Tahoma is a humanist sans-serif typeface designed by Matthew Carter for Microsoft in 1994, known for its legibility for sighted disadvantaged people.

The name Tahoma is derived from the Native American name for Mount Rainier, a prominent feature in the Pacific Northwest region of the United States. This connection reflects the cultural significance and geographical context of the fonts design.

Readers Notes

Readers Notes

Readers Notes

Readers Notes

Readers Notes

www.ingramcontent.com/pod-product-compliance
Lightning Source LLC
Chambersburg PA
CBHW022342040426
42449CB00006B/674